THE SOUND OF MY OWN VOICE

by

VERNON PEARCE

About the author

Vernon Pearce has spent a varied and interesting career in international shipping and logistics, during which time he travelled a great deal. He and his wife Celia also visited many interesting countries on holiday, especially in the Far East.

Vernon retired early from corporate life at the age of 50 and had a second career as a self-employed consultant, his final assignment being Town Initiatives Manager for the market town of Alton in Hampshire, UK, one which he describes as probably the most rewarding of his career. He also became a radio presenter in his spare time.

He has now retired to Spain where he lives in the town of Orba in the north of the Costa Blanca.

This book is a follow-up to his memoirs 'It's a great life if you don't weaken' in which he described his career, some of the places he visited and related many amusing and fascinating anecdotes about his life.

Introduction

This book was written to provide a light-hearted look at the author's experiences of radio presenting on both commercial and hospital radio, undertaken as a part-time interest after his retirement from corporate life. It will hopefully show others who may be interested in following in his footsteps how relatively easy it is to get started in broadcasting and to enjoy sharing your interest in music with others. Whilst it does not purport to be a text book, there are chapters towards the end of the book which offer advice on how to plan and produce radio programmes.

Since 2007 the author, who was once described by one of his colleagues as "the presenter with the voice who can melt a Mars bar at 5 paces", has continued to broadcast from his retirement home on the Costa Blanca in Spain, producing pre-recorded programmes at home and linking to the studio in the UK over the internet via Skype. He has never earned a penny from his broadcasting work but has enjoyed entertaining listeners and meeting some extremely interesting people.

Contents

Contents

First tentative steps in broadcasting

The conversation at dinner parties out here in Spain inevitably turns to what I do with all the time on my hands now I'm retired. I patiently explain that I have many interests, including walking in the mountains with my wife, gardening, working as a mentor for a single-parent charity, singing with a male voice choir, teaching other retired Brits IT skills and, eventually, I get round to admitting that I'm also a radio presenter.

"Oh, so you're a DJ!" they reply, which is why I normally only admit this interest as a last resort. I patiently explain that there is a difference between presenting radio programmes and just playing music. I also have difficulty in persuading our friends that I don't broadcast on any radio stations that they know here in Spain but for Hospital Radio Basingstoke in the UK.

"How on earth did you get involved in being on the

radio?" Well, perhaps that is a good point at which to start my story.

The new lifestyle I embarked upon in the year 2000 in my early fifties (mid-life crisis?) after a lifetime spent in a stressful job in shipping, logistics and computer software, encompassed a desire to try new things. One day, I saw an article in the local newspaper appealing for volunteers to present talk programmes for Wey Valley Radio (WVR) based in Alton, UK, which produced evening programmes on the local Delta FM commercial radio station. I'd had plenty of experience of making formal presentations to management and spent a large part of my career standing up in a wide variety of situations and public speaking, so what could be worse about appearing on the radio, I thought?

Talk about the Environment

I was allowed by the Station Manager to select the subject matter for my monthly, hour-long talk programme and, because the village of Kingsley near

Alton where we lived was threatened at that time with an expanding business park and further sand-quarrying activities, I was becoming increasingly concerned about environmental issues. I therefore named my programme 'Talk about the Environment' and set about finding suitable guests.

I was fortunate to be able to invite into the studio experts from Hampshire Wildlife Trust, Hampshire County Council, English Nature, The National Farmers Union and so on. We discussed the rights and wrongs of building too many houses in rural areas, preserving Hampshire heathlands, protecting otters and many other subjects that I thought would be of interest to the public.

I didn't have to worry about the technical aspects of radio broadcasting at that time, as I had a technical engineer, Neil Ogden, sitting on the other side of the desk. He ensured the programme started on time, that the microphone levels were correct and he kept us on schedule. All I had to do was put intelligent-sounding questions to my guests and control the discussion. I was terrified during the first few months of my new broadcasting career and the 'woodenness' of my presentation was apparent when I listen to those early programmes today.

I also had a major, heart-stopping moment early on, when one of my guests, a District Councillor, called me about an hour before we were due to go on air to say she had a migraine and was unable to take part. I telephoned my mentor and chairman of WVR in a flat panic and he suggested I contacted a local botanist, Dr June Chatfield, who had appeared on previous radio programmes at short notice. I called June who was cooking her supper but agreed that she would turn up and talk about 'something suitable'. I had no time to get any details from her and she arrived at the studio about 10 minutes before her slot whilst I was already on air, clutching a Tupperware container of snail shells and, during a short commercial break, told me that she was going to talk about "the Hampshire cheese snail." I was totally unaware of the existence of this seemingly fictional creature and wasn't sure whether you would eat it or pickle it. However, she was an absolute star and after my rather facile introduction, proceeded to talk non-stop for the allotted 10 minutes, much to my relief.

During those early days, too, my broadcasting mentor, the Chairman of WVR allowed me to use his home studio to edit pre-recorded interviews or recordings of live interviews to be used for 'highlight' programmes. He insisted that these should be ruthlessly edited to remove all pauses and stumbles by either me or the interviewee, to the extent that Dr June Chatfield lost her rather eccentric sounding stammer and began to speak fluently, to the point where she did not recognise herself when she listened to repeats of her interviews with me!

Food and Drink Programme

As the months rolled by the quality of the programmes improved as I gained confidence, relaxed and started to enjoy the sound of my own voice and soon I was offered a second slot. This time

I chose a subject that would be a little more light-hearted and decided on a very different format – 'The Food and Drink Programme'. The press release said -

"A new radio programme about food and drink hits the local airwaves at 8pm on April 15th as part of the regular, Tuesday, Delta Discussion series on Delta FM.

The brain-child of Kingsley man Vernon Pearce, who already presents the Environment Programme on the first Tuesday of the month, the Food and Drink Programme will feature regular contributions from local wine expert Will Grafton and Hampshire Fare Officer, Tim Brock, who will be promoting local food producers. There will also be features on dining-out in local restaurants and pubs, together with recipes and cookery tips and occasional appearances by outside caterers, wedding cake specialists and other experts.

"I hope to provide an interesting and entertaining programme for listeners about eating-in and eating-out, whilst at the same time helping local farmers,

food and drink producers, pubs and restaurants" says Vernon. "Food and drink are much more than a necessity nowadays and our tastes have become more adventurous. We eat out, have takeaways and spend more of our income on food than ever before."

I retained my interest in the local environment and encouraged the participation of local growers and producers, involving local farmer's son Tim Brock, who headed a relatively new project in Hampshire County Council called Hampshire Fare. I also found a wine expert, Will Grafton, who provided his expertise in a regular slot each week talking about wine, together with a cookery expert, Helen Hosker. A regular guest who always talked fluently and interestingly on his subject was American Jerry Schooler, who ran his own country wine-making business called Lurgashall Winery and on one occasion I dedicated a whole one-hour programme to him.

The big difference in this programme was that, in addition to talking about their subjects, the guests were invited to bring along samples to the studio, which we ate and drank on air. With my regular wine expert bringing 2 bottles of wine along to each programme and the fact that I often featured local real-ale breweries, this sometimes led to a very alcoholic evening and some interesting discussions! It was a far more relaxed format and the end result was a much more enjoyable programme.

By now, Delta FM had closed their Alton studio and we were transferred to new studios in Haslemere, Surrey. They also dispensed with engineers and so the presenter had to carry out all the technical functions themselves, something I learned to enjoy and which seemed to improve the slickness of the presentation. However, I now dropped 'Talk about the Environment', as two trips to Haslemere and the time spent getting guests for two programmes was becoming onerous.

My regular guests, Will Grafton, Helen Hosker and Tim Brock, entered into the spirit of the Food and Drink Programme as the weeks went by and started to bring along their own experts and so the breadth and interest level of the subject grew, as did my enjoyment of the experience.

At Haslemere, there was normally a live programme on air before mine started at 8pm but on one particular evening, I arrived to find the studios locked and in darkness. I let myself in with my keys but the burglar alarm had been set and I didn't have the code. I telephoned the Station Manager but the code numbers he gave me failed to silence the alarm. By now it was getting dangerously close to 8pm, the time I was due on air, and so I decided to get my first guests into the studio and start the programme on time after the IRN news. The studio was relatively sound-proof and so the noise of the alarm was barely audible to the listeners. However, about 10 minutes later, I had to carry on like a true professional with a serious discussion on the finer points of that week's selected wine, as fluorescent-jacketed policemen ran backwards and forwards past the studio window, checking the premises for intruders and trying to find someone to turn off the alarm.

Although I was never able to find out the listening figures, the programme was a success and in 2001, I was presented by WVR with the award for 'Best Talk Programme on Delta FM.'

THE FOOD & DRINK PROGRAMME

2004 Schedule

January 20
Wine guide - resident wine expert Will Grafton
Buying fresh local food - Tim Brock, Hampshire Fare Officer
Eating out - Brian Oakes, Rose & Crown Inn, Farringdon
Robin Tyler - Grapevine Delicatessen, Odiham
Tessa Driscoll - Hampshire Farmers' Markets

February 17
Wine guide - resident wine expert Will Grafton, with guest Richard Royds, Haslemere Cellar
Launch of Mr Whitehead Cider Co - Angus Whitehead
Local chef wins Michelin star - Jake Watkins, JSW Restaurant, Petersfield
Find out what Jennifer does with watercress! - Jennifer Laing, Cresson Creative, Alresford

March 16
Wine guide - resident wine expert Will Grafton
Buying fresh local food - Tim Brock, Hampshire Fare Officer with guests Nick Rook-Blackstone, Wylds Farm Partnership, Organic vegetables and Anna Brock from Anna's Kitchen, 'Ready meals' from local produce
Helen Hosker - freelance food expert with guest Rex Goldsmith, fishmonger

April 20
Wine guide - resident wine expert Will Grafton
Buying fresh local food - Tim Brock, Hampshire Fare Officer with guests Will Benson of Applegarth Farm Shop in Grayshott and Rollo Rosetti from Peter Mushrooms
Helen Hosker - food journalist with guest Christina Punchard, Jus de Vie, Haslemere

May 18
Wine guide - resident wine expert Will Grafton
Helen Hosker - food journalist with guest Charles Secrett from Secretts Farm talking about asparagus
Jerry Schooler, Lurgashall Winery
Shon , Rother Valley Organics
Steve Lloyd, Beacon Hill Beer Festival

June 15
Wine guide - resident wine expert Will Grafton
Buying fresh local food - Tim Brock, Hampshire Fare Officer
Carola Brown, Ballards Brewery, Petersfield
Helen Hosker - food journalist with guest Grant Roffey, Leehouse Farm
Ann Sherburn Hall - Headley Fine Foods

Typical schedule for the Food and Drink Programme

Expanding my horizons with Hospital Radio

Meanwhile, my Technical Manager in the early days at Delta FM, Neil Ogden, invited me to join Hospital Radio Basingstoke (HRB), where he was Programme Controller. This was a completely different environment and in addition to requiring me to learn a whole new computer operating system and the mastery of more technical equipment, I had to visit my potential listeners in person – patients and nursing staff at the North Hampshire Hospital (NHH) in Basingstoke, UK – before going on air in order to collect requests.

I was given a two-hour live slot from 8 - 10pm on a weekday evening and presented my first show on Thursday 29th August 2003 with requests, live information and ad-libs, as well as gaffs! My signature tune was 'True' by Spandau Ballet, a favourite of mine, which was a quiet track and set the theme for my programme.

The technical skills involved in presenting a live music request programme, single handed, were much more demanding. Music tracks had to be found either on a computerised database, in a library of CDs or on vinyl albums. The mixing desk incorporated two CD decks, the old vinyl record turntable, announcer and guest microphones, a telephone link and of course, the computer playout software, on which I also had to cue-up pre-recorded jingles, programme trailers and information 'carts' as they were called. This harked back to the days in commercial radio when the adverts were recorded on 8-track cartridges, which were pushed into players at the appropriate moment. The other challenge was to fit the programme around 'commercial breaks' every quarter of an hour and the IRN news bulletins, which had to be played out exactly on the hour from a live satellite link.

I found the format far more enjoyable and rewarding, although it was very difficult to get any feedback in the form of phone calls to the studio. However, something happened soon after I started that not only gave me a tremendous amount of satisfaction but also provided a great publicity opportunity for the station.

We received an e-mail from a lady called Noreen Jonczyk in the United States, asking us to play a request for a patient, 66-year old Nancy Best, who was also from the US and who, when she was in the UK on holiday with her husband, was taken ill and admitted to the High Dependency Unit at the Basingstoke hospital. Her cousin Noreen, whom she hadn't seen for 25 years, heard about her misfortune and figured that Nancy could do with cheering up. Cousin Noreen, who was also in her late 60s and by her own admission not very computer literate, had no idea where Basingstoke was or how to contact the hospital. However, she searched the internet and found HRB's web site, from where she was able to e-mail the station and ask us to play Frank Sinatra's "High Hopes" - chosen, she said, because she and Nancy were "teenagers of the fifties" and she had "high hopes of Nancy's recovery!"

I played the request the next day on my early evening show and Nancy was thrilled to hear the song and the 'get well' message from her cousin across the Atlantic. By the next day, Nancy's daughter in the US had been told the news and had e-mailed cousin Noreen to tell her the request had been played. Nancy was transferred a few weeks later from the HDU to a general ward and when I visited her there, she said that the request had "knocked her socks off!"

We had another e-mail from Noreen back in the US saying, "I cannot express thanks enough to you for being so kind and courteous to us "Yanks". I'm sure by you visiting and showing concern that it perked up my cousin. I'm sure anyone that's been in hospital as long as she has and especially being an ocean away from home must get despondent. With the Thanksgiving holidays coming up, that compounds it." Noreen included with her message a special poem about Thanksgiving, which I read out on air on the appropriate day.

I went to see Nancy again a few weeks later and she was out of bed, sitting up and eating her Sunday lunch and, shortly afterwards, she was released from hospital and flew back home to the US. The story had a happy ending on Christmas Eve with an e-mail from Nancy herself, wishing everyone at HRB a Merry Christmas and saying that she was well on the way to recovery. "Thanks for doing the piece about me and the request from my cousin Noreen....Take care and keep up the good programme. You are a part of my best memories of England!"

The story made the local newspaper and shows how the internet and e-mail has shrunk the world. It's also a great example of how hospital radio provides a personal service to the staff and patients whose recovery it often helps.

Sound of Country

Soon I became the Treasurer of HRB and, as my radio presenting skills and experience with HRB grew, I began to feel strongly that the station should be providing a range of entertainment which more closely matched our audience, particularly as most of our presenters were young and their choice of music probably wouldn't satisfy the patients, who were obviously much older.

I therefore convinced the committee to allow me to create a range of different pre-recorded programmes, starting with 'The Sound of Country', featuring my recently–acquired collection of country music that had grown out of my trips to the USA on business and the line dancing that my wife and I had learnt at evening classes in the village where we lived. I went to great lengths to avoid what I thought was the more clichèd Country and Western music and the trailer for my programme invited listeners to -

"Join me, Vernon Pearce, at 7 o'clock on Sunday evening for the Sound of Country here on Hospital Radio Basingstoke - an hour of modern American country music featuring artists such as Alan Jackson and Shania Twain, Leann Rimes and Tricia Yearwood - and even if you think you don't like country music, listen in 'cos you might just find you enjoy the Sound of Country here on Hospital Radio Basingstoke."

At Christmas I even recorded a festive special, featuring carols and other seasonal songs recorded by country singers.

The 'Sound of Country' programmes were so successful that an updated series is still being broadcast regularly today.

I followed up that series with programmes of quieter, more romantic music – 'Late Night Love' - now renamed and still being broadcast as 'The Love Songs Hour'. This goes out at midnight and contains very little chat from the presenter.

Smooth Jazz and Sound of the '40s

During my visits to the USA on business I had not only acquired an interest in country music but also that of saxophonist Kenny G, whose CDs I had begun to collect and also been lucky enough to attend one of his concerts at the Royal Albert Hall. Also, in my search for a theme song and standby music tracks for my talk programmes on Delta FM, I had acquired an interest in 'Smooth Jazz'. Once again, this inspired another series of programmes, which I re-recorded many years later when I moved to Spain and met a very talented saxophonist.

By now I was getting a taste for pre-recorded programmes in which I featured my own tastes in music and which I could make in my own time. Soon I had the idea of appealing more directly to the elderly patients in the hospital by creating 'The Sound of the '40s', borrowing CDs from my mum and dad and linking the tracks with material I researched on the internet. The trailer for this series went along these lines -

"Hi, this is Vernon Pearce, inviting you to join me for the Sound of the '40s - a nostalgic look at the era of big band sound, music hall and great names such as Bing Crosby and Nat King Cole, Deanna Durbin and Vera Lynn and featuring the great piano playing of Charlie Kunz. Let me help you re-live those memories of WW2, back to the days of air raids and rationing, jitterbugging and nylon stockings! So join me soon for the Sound of the '40s here on Hospital Radio Basingstoke."

Once again, I produced a Christmas special, featuring some seasonal songs of the period such as White Christmas and some rare recordings of radio broadcasts to American troops in the UK and Germany in the '40s. An artist who featured regularly in these programmes was, of course, Glenn Miller and so I produced a one hour special called 'The Glenn Miller Story,' telling listeners a little about the life of the American jazz musician, arranger, composer and one of the most famous big band leaders in the swing era - many say of all time.

Your Song and Grumpy Old Men

I was becoming quite skilled by this time at interviewing guests in the studio for my talk programmes on Delta FM and so I decided that we at HRB should create our own version of Desert Island Discs with a programme called 'Your Song'. In this series, I interviewed hospital managers, doctors and staff, together with local celebrities such as the mayor, the manager of the Sports Centre, a judge and on one occasion, received on air the money raised by Dummer Golf Club for HRB as their charity of the year. In between discussions about their careers, interests, etc. I played their choice of music. At one point I was a 'victim' on my own programme, interviewed by the soon-to-be-Chairman of HRB and a close friend to this day, Marilyn Price.

One of the people I interviewed for this series was a recently-joined member of HRB and someone I was to develop a close friendship with, Brian Starman. He was about the same age as me and although he and his wife Anita were heavily involved in amateur dramatics with the nearby Hook Players and he had the confidence needed for radio presenting, Brian was terrified of the technical operations involved and was seriously considering resigning from the station. The 'Your Song' programme in which he appeared was a very good one and we 'sparked off each other' immediately.

We therefore decided to produce a series together called 'Grumpy Old Men', modelled on the TV series of the same name, in which we would moan about the unfairness of life, bureaucracy and the things that really annoyed us, as well as playing our own choice of music. Our notes prepared for the station management at the time described the series as -

"An hour-long pre-recorded programme of music and talk, presented by Vernon Pearce and Brian Starman. The 'talk' will major on things that annoy us, such as queues at banks and post offices, bank charges, unsolicited phone calls, junk mail etc. Wherever possible, we will suggest solutions, e.g. how to get your name removed from mailing lists, how to get cheaper banking, pay your TV licence by direct debit to avoid queuing at PO, how to save fuel/electricity, etc. We'll try and avoid race, politics and other sensitive areas that might bring HRB into disrepute. However, we WILL be 'grumpy'!"

I was responsible for the technical operations, leaving Brian free to relax and be himself on air. It was a great success and we recorded a series of six programmes, stopping at a point when we felt that we might become repetitive if we continued.

Outside broadcasts

In 2004 I started a three year contract as the Town Initiatives Manager for Alton, UK. My role was to promote the town centre and one of my priority tasks was to organise events that would attract people into the town and increase footfall in the shops and pubs. Between 2004 and 2007 I organised many successful Classic Car Shows, a Civil War Weekend, '40s Days and many other events. I saw these occasions as an ideal opportunity for HRB to widen the scope of its programming and invited them along to interview participants and capture the noise and atmosphere of the day for later broadcast in special programmes. As the organiser of these events I often found myself on the other side of the microphone and an interviewee for a change!

I also took part in several outside broadcasts for HRB in my role as a presenter, including the Big Balloon Festival in Basingstoke and several Golf Days at Dummer Golf Club near Basingstoke.

On Easter Sunday 2005, HRB broadcast from Basingstoke's living history museum – Milestones. Sarah Beattie, Harry Robinson, Dave Leonard and I walked around the museum, talking to the staff and the visitors and watching the special events and even made use of the museum's own studio. The interviews were broadcast later in the day and during a special show on Easter Monday.

HRB grows

In addition to radio presenting, I was also involved with the management of the station, serving on the committee as Treasurer from 2003-2006 and getting involved in the all-important task of fund-raising. I took part in charity golf days and a sponsored bike ride to the most northerly hospital radio station in Scotland, although I hasten to add that we rode static exercise bikes and never left the warmth and comfort of Festival Place shopping centre in Basingstoke, raising £1,704 in the process! We also did numerous 'tin rattles' outside supermarkets, in shopping centres and at the front of the hospital, where I would often be dressed in a yellow chicken outfit.

The station went from strength to strength, winning a number of Hospital Broadcasting Association (HBA) awards and in 2016 was nominated for a record seven awards. Soon after my wife and I retired to Spain, HRB replaced their ageing and cramped portacabin, under the project management of Brian Starman, with a much larger and more modern one, providing a smart new suite of studios and offices.

Before I left for Spain, I was privileged to be made an Honorary Member of Hospital Radio Basingstoke.

Broadcasting from the sun!

In 2007, my wife and I sold our home in Hampshire and retired to the Costa Blanca in Spain. The changes in the pace of life, the climate and the culture were enormous and we quickly settled in and adapted to our new life in the sun. This was also an opportunity to take up new hobbies and pursue new interests and to explore the beautiful mountains and the Spanish villages around us here in Orba in the north of the Costa Blanca.

Some years previously, an HRB presenter who worked in the North Hampshire Hospital, Andrew McCormick, had returned to his native New Zealand and was presenting a programme called 'Postcard from New Zealand', recorded at home and sent to HRB via the internet. Neil Ogden, HRB's Programme Controller, suggested I might do the same. Thus was born 'Postcard from Spain' and a whole new era of broadcasting from my new home in Spain.

The format of 'Postcard from Spain' was a weekly magazine programme, mixing local news items with music from the 70s and 80s, selected at random by the station's playout software from its music database. I was sent a playlist of the selected songs, jingles and information breaks and I then recorded the speech links, which were sent to the studio over the internet and dropped in at the appropriate points. In this way, I knew what music would be played and at what time and so was able to make my links sound as if I was broadcasting live. The programme introduction would go something like this -

"It's just after 7 o'clock on this Friday evening and this is Vernon Pearce saying buenes tardes – good evening - and welcome to another edition of Postcard from Spain. I'll be keeping you company for the next hour, bringing you some of the best music of the 70s and 80s, together with news and views from sunny Spain. In tonight's programme............"

I have always been a keen cook and when we retired to Spain, I was able to explore a whole new Mediterranean cuisine, using local fresh vegetables and ingredients. I therefore decided to incorporate a regular 'recipe of the week' spot into my programme. The recipe was read out towards the end of the programme and for listeners unable to write down all the details, a special web page was provided for me on HRB's website to promote 'Postcard from Spain' and allow listeners to look up the recipes incorporated in the programme. This web page still exists and if you are interested in cooking something with a Mediterranean flavour, have a look at www.hrbasingstoke.co.uk/postcardfromspain.

After a few years, I reduced the frequency of 'Postcard from Spain' to monthly, as other interests I had cultivated in my retirement began to make demands on my time. I also became disillusioned with the random music tracks that the playout system was selecting for me. I therefore decided to make the complete one-hour programme myself and dropped the '70s/'80s theme for my favourite music, albeit my tastes are very much from that era. I also dropped the regular recipe spot, which I decided on reflection probably didn't appeal to my mainly bed-bound audience.

On the subject of being bed-bound, in 2011 I needed an operation on my right foot and as a result was confined to bed for a week. This coincided with my monthly 'Postcard from Spain' programme but in true 'the show must go on' style, I recorded the programme from bed!

Meanwhile, another fellow HRB presenter, Paul Lefeuvre, associated for many years with Treloar Hospital Radio in Alton, was also producing 'Postcard from France' from his holiday home in that country and 'Postcard from Switzerland' when visiting his son's home there.

The Lunchbox

One of the many interests with which my wife and I

became involved soon after arriving in Spain was amateur dramatics - something neither of us had dabbled in before but which proved to be great fun and a way to make friends in the expat community here. A fellow member of the Careline Theatre group which we joined was Andy Crabb, who, with his wife Sonia, had spent much of their lives teaching in South Africa. Andy 'hid his light under a bushel', as they say, but I eventually discovered that he wrote short stories in his spare time. Andy gave me one of the books of stories that he had published and I was amazed at the quality of his writing and how entertaining the stories were. I was keen to share these with a wider audience and thought that hospital radio would be an ideal vehicle.

So I came up with the idea of 'The Lunchbox', a magazine programme which would be broadcast during the lunchtime consisting of short stories, anecdotes, interesting facts about the hospital and Basingstoke, etc. The way in which it was constructed as a pre-recorded series was very complex. I recorded all the links and these were put in separate folders for short stories, generic links, specific-day links, trailers and sweepers etc. The idea was that the playout software would compile an almost infinite variety of daily programmes, which would appear to be specific and live. I also searched the internet and found a very catchy song called 'It's lunchtime' from a children's TV show to be the theme tune for the programme.

In order to provide more short stories of the right length and a greater variety of subject matter, I contacted the local U3A, who had a writers' circle, where I found a couple of budding authors and poets whose material I could use. I also persuaded one of them to recite her own work on air, which also provided a different voice to give relief from mine.

The programme became a daily feature in HRB's schedule for a while and was still being broadcast in 2013 and 2014 but the playout software seemed not to be random enough, which led to some stories and items being repeated too often.

Live linkups

I shall deal in a later chapter with the way in which
advances in technology during my time in
broadcasting have greatly improved the standard of
our output and led to huge improvements in
programming. A couple of examples in which I was
involved illustrate this well.

In 2012 HRB celebrated its 40th birthday by
broadcasting an all-day, live programme and invited
back many presenters from the past, some of whom
had gone on to have successful careers in
broadcasting with the BBC and commercial radio
stations. I was asked to take part in a special phone-in
on an afternoon programme hosted by Kestrel FM's
Steve Fox. Also appearing in this link was Andrew
McCormick, presenter of 'Postcard from New
Zealand' fame, all the way from his home down
under. Via a Skype VOIP link, the three of us chatted
live on air and, listening to the recording of the
programme, we could all have been sitting in the
same studio in Basingstoke. Andrew sounded very

tired, however, as it was 02:00 in Auckland!

Also in 2012, HRB presenter Chris Bounds attempted to broadcast live for 2012 minutes, or 33.5 hours, raising money for the station. I joined him on air on two occasions to try and fill some of his programming time, again via Skype. During the first of these links, Chris admitted that he often referred to me on air when publicising or linking into my programmes as "the presenter with the voice who can melt a Mars bar at 5 paces"!

I occasionally appear on other presenters' programmes, including a fortnightly 'Europe' slot on Christine Rowley's 'Music on Demand' programme, providing some added interest about life in Spain, talking about where I live, local restaurants and food and showing HRB's technical skills, which even many commercial radio stations cannot match. I also act as independent 'draw-master' on Neil Ogden's 'Sound of Sunday' sometimes, selecting the winner of the weekly, Sainsbury's gift voucher. I also like to take part in link-ups with presenters who have given up their time to do live programmes on Christmas Day.

The Best of....

The availability of more spare time and the desire to make greater use of my music database led me in 2016 to develop another idea for a new series of programmes. The format of 'The Best of...' is an hour-long programme of one artist's music - hits and album tracks - accompanied by information about the artist and the tracks played. The series, first broadcast on 8th April 2016, features some of 'the greats' such as Phil Collins, Stevie Wonder, Rod Stewart and Elton John, together with groups such as Abba, Bee Gees and the Eagles. Once again, the era I chose to select these artists from represents the age range of the listeners in the NHH. I had an enormous amount of fun selecting the best tracks from each artist's albums and researching on the internet facts about their early lives and careers. 'The Best of ...' is currently filling a gap in the programme schedule on Friday evenings.

Live musicians

One of the joys of living on the Costa Blanca is the variety of live music we are able to listen to, with many bars offering free entertainment in the evenings to attract customers, both residents and tourists, to their terraces. In 2015 a saxophonist called Frank Abrams from Swindon, UK, made his first appearance on the local circuit. My wife and I were very impressed with his musical abilities and it reminded me of my love for Kenny G and smooth jazz. He soon established a name for himself and returned again the next summer to take up permanent residence locally.

By now I felt that my 'Smooth Jazz' programme, which had been running for 12 years, was sounding a little tired and so I embarked on a re-make, utilising some of Frank Abram's music and some interviews with him. He proved to be very relaxed in front of the microphone and added another dimension to the links between tracks. This time I made a series of complete one-hour programmes instead of just voice-tracking.

The first programme was aired on 25th June 2016 and is currently being broadcast on HRB at 23:00 on a Saturday evening.

At about the same time as Frank Abrams was helping me with the new 'Smooth Jazz' programme, another British artist appeared in a one-off concert at a local restaurant, whilst she was in Spain on holiday. Singer-songwriter from Bedford, UK, Danni Nicholls had a refreshing sound and some catchy songs, described as 'Americana' but with echoes of the modern American country music I play in the 'Sound of Country' series. I was lucky enough to arrange for Frank to bring Danni to my villa for an hour, during which we recorded a series of sound bites about her life and songs, even recording her playing a live version of one of the songs from her latest album. There was sufficient material, together with songs from her albums, to enable me to make a very entertaining one-hour special, first broadcast on 5th June 2016 and which has now been added to the rest of the 'Sound of Country' series, currently being broadcast on a Sunday evening.

...and now for something completely different

Another new venture for me in my retirement (surely
the midlife crisis has passed by now?) was to join a
choir - the Costa Blanca Male Voice Choir to be
exact. I hadn't sung in public, apart from the
occasional, embarrassing karaoke appearance, since
my school days. However, I had been so 'blown away'
with the sound this choir made when I attended one
of their concerts that I was persuaded by my wife to
join them. After two years of singing in concerts with
them and sometimes joint concerts with other choirs, I
heard that we were to share the stage with the
Basingstoke Ladies Choir. I could not believe this
coincidence, as I had not been involved in any way
with the planning - the choir were on a group holiday
in nearby Benidorm.

I arranged for our sound technician, Brian Norbury, to
record the whole concert, enabling us to hopefully
capture some good quality tracks for a current CD we
were trying to compile and for me to compile a radio
special to be broadcast on HRB. The result was an

excellent recording, which was made into a one-hour special programme, complete with its own trailer and a slideshow set to music on Facebook. The programme enabled the ladies of the choir and their families, friends and followers in UK to listen to the concert, broadcast on HRB over the internet on 11th June 2016.

Delta Local Radio

Delta FM, with whom I had started my radio career, was eventually purchased by the Tindle Newspaper Group and in 2010, it's Haslemere studio was closed down and the station merged with Kestrel FM, Basingstoke. An experienced radio presenter and producer who was known to some of the ex-WVR and Delta staff, Alan Rowett, tried to keep the Delta name alive and started up an internet-based station called Delta Local Radio. As my contribution to this project I made versions of my 'Postcard from Spain' and 'Sound of Country' programmes using newly-created jingles and sweepers which he sent me. The station ceased broadcasting after a while unfortunately as insufficient money was available to finance the operation.

Radio Vall de Pop

This was the reason for the failure of another project which I tried to get off the ground soon after moving to Spain. We live in a mountainous area in which FM signals are sometimes weak. This was particularly true of the Vall de Pop or Jalon Valley as it is sometimes known. I met a local DJ called Tony Dean, who had the idea of starting up a local internet radio station to serve the area. Over a number of months, we studied the feasibility of this, including the costs of renting sufficient internet capacity to broadcast and the various licences we would need. This gave us an indication of the advertising revenue we would need to finance the station, which is where the project foundered. There are just too many stations chasing a limited amount of advertising budget from local companies and so, with both of us being retired and not wanting to squander our pensions on a dream, the idea was dropped.

Mr PA Man

Being a radio presenter often leads to requests to do PA work, because having a good 'radio voice' and experience in using a microphone means you will come across well at your local fete, reading out the raffle prizes at the firm's dinner dance, etc!

Laverstoke Park

My broadcasting activities on Delta FM and my role as Town Initiatives Manager in Alton raised my public profile and in July 2005 I was asked if I would be interested in providing the PA for an Open Day at Laverstoke Park, home of ex-F1 racing driver champion Jody Scheckter. He has made a second career in organic farming and on his extensive estate near Basingstoke, UK, he keeps water buffalo, sheep, pigs, wild boar, other animals and poultry, has his own butcher's shop and was even planning to add an organic micro-brewery. When I visited him to discuss the terms of my day's engagement, he proudly showed me round the several farms he has bought and combined over the years to make the extensive estate that he likes to throw open to the public each year.

My wife Celia accompanied me on the Saturday and we were excited to discover that TV chef James Martin was a guest and that our base for the PA equipment was in the very barn in which he was giving cookery demonstrations. At one stage, we helped him out when his own PA equipment had problems and, as a result, had several chats with him. We found him a very friendly and unassuming man, unspoilt by his fame.

I say 'helped him out with his PA' but we were hardly qualified to do so. When we arrived at the main farmyard in the morning, the PA equipment had already been installed by a contractor the previous day and there was no-one to show us how it worked. Everyone was running around like the proverbial headless chickens and we were expected to start announcements immediately. I established how to switch it on and started playing some background music but it was barely audible through the various speakers, which were placed strategically around the public areas - even at full volume. The speakers were Bose and their 'rugged' appearance seemed appropriate for the location. It wasn't until some helpful member of the public whispered to me that I would get a better result if I took the covers off, that I realised what the cause of the problem was!

After lunch, Jody Scheckter started the engine of the original F1 car in which he had clinched the driver's championship in 1979. It was an event for which I had to commentate and I interviewed Jody, his mechanic and then James Martin. Standing alongside the F1 car as Jody revved the engine was an ear-shattering experience.

The day ended with an invitation for Celia and I to attend a special barbecue held for all the staff on the farm and those involved with the event, at which we enjoyed buffalo burgers.

Alton Show

Staying with the agricultural theme, I was then offered the job of commentating at the Alton Show in July 2006 and again in 2007. It was the very weekend of Laverstoke Park's Open Day, which meant I was unable to return to the event for a second year. Instead, I passed the baton to one of my HRB colleagues, Andy K.

The Alton Show was one of the major agricultural shows in the area and a completely different event. I was based for the day in a glass-fronted, commentator's caravan in the main arena, scene of the heavy horse display, the horse and carriage judging, tractor parade, the main parade of prize-winning animals and, of course, all the exciting arena events, such as motorcycle display teams, wild west riding displays and one year, the arrival of the Red Devils parachute display team.

In addition to commentating on all these different activities, I acted as the link man, publicising activities taking place elsewhere in the showground and providing public service announcements about lost children (and parents!), lost keys and purses and a hundred and one other things. I was very grateful for my wife Celia's help on these occasions, when she acted as my 'secretary', dealt with enquiries and provided me with the relevant notes and information.

We had some amusing situations and I remember the woman who asked if we could announce that she had found a budgerigar. Intrigued as to how a budgie would be flying around the Alton showground, it eventually transpired that she meant at her home in Alton and she thought the show would be a good place to appeal to its owner!

The main arena was where most of the action took place and, being the central figure as it were, I was held responsible for everything that happened …. and went wrong. The show is organized by an association of farmers, landowners and other well-meaning folk of the countryside. That it runs as well as it does is something of a miracle and the first time I did the job, communication was somewhat lacking. Sometimes, the first thing I would know of an event starting was the arrival of the participants at the arena entrance.

When the main parade of animals started to enter the arena, I had not received the results of the judging from the Secretary's tent and had no idea who the various participants were. My commentary was therefore completely ad-lib and probably sounded very unprofessional. The prize-giving took place in front of the members' enclosure and I announced the winners' names but when the President stepped forward to present the prize for the best bull, it's owner let forth a tirade of abuse and criticism against me as the commentator. He was most offended that I had not mentioned his name or that of his precious animal and was completely unaware of the chaos that had been taking place behind the scenes. I took the abuse without comment but was indignant afterwards that I should have been placed in such an invidious position. I was adamant that I would not be available to perform the role the next year. However, the farmer was told that his behaviour was unacceptable and the incident was smoothed over, whilst I was offered more professional assistance the following year from experts able to talk with more knowledge about cattle, heavy horses and so on.

Whilst the fee for my services was very good, it was nevertheless a very stressful day, with little chance for much of a rest from the time we arrived at about 08:30 until the proceedings ended about 17:30. The job was made a little easier by having constantly on hand the engineer who installed all the PA equipment throughout the showground; he was always very professional and I used his services at some of my events in the town centre.

Announcer at Kingsley Benefit Fund Fetes

When I first became involved with the organisation of the village fete in Kingsley, near Alton, where we lived, the PA had always been provided by Paul Lefuerve, one of the founder members of Treloar

Hospital radio and a fellow presenter on WVR, Delta FM and later at HRB. When I started organising events as Town Initiatives Manager in Alton, I used Paul's services for the Classic Car show and the '40s Day and the partnership worked extremely well. Paul not only provided the music and made announcements but toured the stalls and talked to members of the public.

Paul is married to Liz who is French and they have another home in southern France, where they spend much of the summer. There were some years therefore, when he was unavailable for the fete but on those occasions, he kindly loaned me his equipment and I became the announcer for the day. This was another opportunity for me to gain experience and I had great fun, because it was a much more relaxed environment than the Alton Show.

In addition to selecting my own taste in music, I announced the winners of the prize draw, fronted some impromptu auctions, commentated on the tug of war and children's races and generally publicised all the stalls and activities taking place. It was a great privilege to be asked in 2007, just as we were about to leave the UK for Spain, to open the fete and rather strange to be 'on the other side of the microphone'!

Other MC duties

I am frequently asked to be MC at functions for organisations with which I am involved and whilst I am often happy to oblige, the downside is that I often have to sacrifice time I should be spending with my wife or with friends and fellow guests at the dinner table ... and where am I when it comes to that all-important dance with the wife? Supervising the raffle prize draw or liaising with the band!

So please remember when you say to someone, "You're good at speaking in public aren't you? Would you like to draw the raffle prize winners at this year's Christmas dinner dance?"

In 2013 the Careline Theatre group, which my wife Celia and I had joined shortly after retiring to Spain, put on a production called 'Those Good Old Days' and I landed my dream role - that of MC Leonard Sachs. I thoroughly enjoyed playing his OTT character and copying his mellifluous and wordy introductions, opening the show, complete with my gavel and white gloves -

"Good evening, ladies and gentlemen! Welcome to the Careline Theatre. Tonight, we have a veritable cornucopia of entertainment for your delectation .... and to start us off, we have a super, sensitive, soiree of songs ..... I give you our own .... our very own, the colourful and radiant .... Careline Company of Those Good Old Days!"

Alton Town Initiatives Manager interviewed by HRB presenter Rob Green

Broadcasting from bed

Interviewing Jody Scheckter and James Martin at Laverstoke Park Open Day

Appearing as MC Leonard Sachs in 'Those Good Old Days'

Making a radio programme

The following chapters are intended to provide some guidance for beginners on how to go about making a radio programme. This is not a text book and the object is simply to detail some of the steps that I, as a methodical person, have found useful.

Equipment for broadcasting from home

I have only two pieces of equipment for recording radio programmes at home - a reasonable quality condenser microphone - a Samson Q1U on a desk stand, price £33 from Amazon - and recording software - Sound Forge Studio, £45 and available online from Sony. No mixing desk is necessary as the software enables me to set sound levels for voice and music and to mix the two at whatever levels I choose, fading music in and out, talking over the top of songs and so on. The software is extremely good for editing speech and enables me to sound professional and word perfect, even on a bad day!

Unless you are a perfectionist, it really isn't necessary to build a sound-proofed studio in your home. Spanish villas are notoriously echoey, with tiled floors and very little soft furnishings to deaden the sound. Believe it or not, when I first started recording 'Postcard from Spain', I placed the microphone inside the linen cupboard! However, nowadays I've dispensed with such idiosyncrasies and, providing I wait until my wife is not vacuuming or running the washing machine, I can avoid any need for sound-deadening. We are very lucky to live in a peaceful valley, far from main roads and with no low-flying aircraft.

A good broadband link is also necessary for sending the completed, pre-recorded programmes to your Programme Controller using Dropbox, YouSendIt, Hightail or other file transfer software. My one-hour programmes usually exceed 100Mb in size, which can take a while to download to HRB in Basingstoke.

Planning - Know your audience

The very first point to establish, whether you are making a talk or a music programme is –

Who are your audience going to be?
What is their age range?
What time of the day will your programme be broadcast?

For example, it's no good playing hip-hop music to a hospital ward full of patients in their 60s and 70s and no point in having a studio guest talking about pensions on a university radio station! Tailor your programme to what you think your listeners will enjoy but also keep to music genres or topics that you are comfortable with; your weaknesses will soon come to light when you are 'live' in front of the microphone. Concentrate, at least at the beginning as I did, on your favourite areas and those where you are most knowledgeable.

Why do you need to think about your audience? All commercial radio stations depend on advertising revenue and it's likely they will be competing for the limited budgets of potential clients against local newspapers and magazines, particularly the free press, as well as other local radio stations and even TV. Audience figures from the official body responsible for measuring radio audiences in the UK, RAJAR, will almost certainly play a big part in their decision whether to take advertising space on your radio station and in particular during your programme and will make the job of your sales team a lot easier. In the case of hospital radio, patients will make more requests during programmes they enjoy listening to or with presenters they feel most comfortable with ..... and it is request numbers which are normally taken as a measure of success at the end of the day.

Once you have established your audience, you can then start to draw up a shortlist of potential studio guests or compile music playlists.

Planning - pre-recorded music programmes

Live programmes are much more stressful because they are, by their very nature, 'live' and very time-specific. However, if you are producing a series of pre-recorded programmes, like my 'Smooth Jazz' or 'Sound of Country', you need to consider carefully how they are likely to be scheduled. I have found that it is much better to make them 'vanilla', in other words not time or day specific, giving the Programme Controller more freedom to fit you into his schedule. We will discuss later the making of trailers which can be used to publicise your particular slot.

Another difference between live and pre-recorded programmes is that, whilst the former are more stressful - you *have* to finish on time in order go into the news bulletin on the hour, for example - pre-recorded or voice-tracked programmes are made to be 56.5 minutes or so long and the playout software will fill any spare time with jingles or sweepers. I always find it easier to finish my pre-recorded music programmes with a track that can be faded out, rather than try to juggle my schedule to fit exactly into the 56.5 minutes.

If you are preparing a series of programmes, create a playlist of all the music to be used throughout the series to ensure that, unless you deliberately plan to play 'two in a row' by a particular artist, you get sufficient variety into each individual programme. Then create a running order of the music for each individual programme - I find it helpful to retrieve all my music tracks and create a skeleton for each programme first, adding the speech links later. (I'll be dealing with the recording software I use and how this can help you later.)

I then decide on how many speech links I'm going to include - eight to ten is usually sufficient, so that the listener doesn't get tired of your voice and can listen to the music without too many interruptions! The length of these links should also be limited - better to impart a small amount of useful but interesting information, than to bore the listener. The next step is to prepare scripts or notes for each of these links, although make sure you read these in a casual way, in order not to make it obvious that you are doing so. (I will deal later with where to find material for your programmes.)

Make sure you include jingles or sweepers between music tracks and speech links, as well as reminding the listener once or twice during the programme who they are listening to - they may have just tuned in or nodded off during one of your rather long speech links! To explain the terminology, a sweeper is a short, pre-recorded sound bite, generally 20 seconds or less, used by radio stations as a segue between songs to give a brief station identifier or promo - *"You're listening to HRB, broadcasting 24 hours a day on Patientline".* A jingle is a short song or tune advertising the station, a forthcoming radio programme or a service announcement.

Create a running order for your whole programme, taking into account news bulletins and information or commercial breaks, remembering to introduce yourself as soon as possible after the start of the programme. Also remember to allow time to sign-off at the end, reminding the listener when he or she can hear the next one in the series. However, if you are making your series 'vanilla', it will only be - *"I'll be back tomorrow/next week/month with another ...."*

Planning - music and general live programmes

Much of the preparation for pre-recorded programmes applies to live programmes as well; very few presenters have the skill or experience of the late, great Terry Wogan in being able to turn up at the studio at 5 minutes to six every morning and present a two or three hour programme 'off the cuff'.

With live programmes, the advice is to be prepared to constantly review your schedule, be very time conscious, improvise where necessary, be flexible, sound professional and above all, keep calm! It's always a good idea to segue into the next programme and for presenters to mutually support each other with gentle plugs.

Planning - talk programmes

When inviting guests to talk on your programme, try to select those who you know are knowledgeable about their subject, interesting to listen to and reasonably fluent. It will be hard work if you find within seconds of starting the interview that you are going to have to continually prompt your guest or that getting them to talk is like getting blood out of a stone.

Research their subject so that you sound reasonably knowledgeable and create a list of sufficient questions or topics to ensure you don't run out of things to say. Conversely, decide in advance roughly how long you are going to allocate to each guest and don't let them overrun - control the interview but don't stifle your guest! Don't try to make yourself look clever or belittle your guest - you may find people reluctant to appear on your programme if you gain yourself a bad reputation. Remember - the guest will probably be as nervous as, if not more so, than you.

Programme material

Unless you are making talk programmes, you will certainly need access to a large library of music. When I started broadcasting with HRB, we had a physical library of vinyl records (mainly 33rpm) and CDs but increasingly, we were building up a database of computerised tracks, catalogued by a piece of software called Myriad. Over the past 10 to 15 years I have been copying (or 'ripping') all my personal CDs onto a computer hard drive to make cataloguing and using these tracks much easier. All my pre-recorded programmes are now made quickly and easily using this database of almost 25Gb of over 200 albums.

At this point I should mention music copyright. In the UK, digitally copying a CD onto your computer is strictly speaking illegal but no record company is going to pursue a private individual if they are using it for their own pleasure, rather than to share with other people or for commercial gain. Using copyrighted music in a public broadcast is also illegal, unless the broadcaster has a PPL licence, which HRB has and pays for each year. You can get further information here – www.ppluk.com.

There are ways of supplementing your personal record collection by subscribing to on-line music databases such as Spotify or Last.fm and I understand the former is used quite often now by HRB for its 'Music on Demand' programmes, making it much easier to satisfy patients' requests.

Over the years I have compiled an extensive file of miscellaneous material for use in radio programmes - anecdotes, jokes, facts, truisms, etc. taken from the internet, books, newspapers and magazines for use as fill-ins. My research for specialist music programmes takes me to online services such as Wikipedia and to artists' websites, biographies and so on.

However, my most useful tool is a website called www.everyhit.com, which enables me to inform the listener when a song was a hit, how high it climbed in the UK charts, how many weeks it stayed there and who originally recorded it or who also had a hit with it. In other words, how to come across as a right, music clever-dick!

Recording using Sound Forge

Once you have a list of the music you are going to play, a running order for the programme and scripts for the voice links, it's time to start recording - this is the exciting bit!

I won't go into detail on how to use this software as there is plenty of on-screen help, suffice it to say that it is simple to use and very 'visual'. You create a new file for your programme, copying and pasting in existing music tracks, jingles and sweepers, recording new speech tracks and assembling them in the order you wish. You can watch the programme beginning to build on the screen as a series of waves and the time is shown above the wave ribbon on the screen, reminding you of your progress.

Editing your speech links is very simple and you can

delete coughs and splutters, ums and ahhs etc. later - just keep talking, repeating any parts which you get wrong and go back and polish it up at the end. I find it useful to save my speech links separately, rather than just paste them into the programme, in case I need to go back and rebuild the programme or use those links again in the future.

There are fade in/fade out functions and you can paste in your speech links over the top of music at whatever volume you wish, enabling you to talk over a track. You can insert silence and do lots of other things I've never really understood the need for but which I'm sure broadcasting geeks would find infinitely satisfying!

When you have finished recording, listened back to it and ensure it is what you want your listeners to hear, use the Sound Forge function to equalise the sound level for the whole programme. Finally, don't forget to save a copy before sending it off to your Programme Controller.

You will improve the quality of your broadcast by listening to the programmes as often as possible and being very self-critical. I still do this, even after nearly 15 years, and am always thinking how the listener is thinking - am I interesting? Do I talk too much? Speak over the end of music tracks? It isn't only the technical quality which is important but the entertainment level of the programme.

Trailers and publicity

All your best efforts in making the perfect radio programme will have been wasted if no-one listens to it and so making a trailer to promote your programme is a very important function that is often neglected by presenters.

The trailer should be bright and cheerful, lasting about 30 seconds, telling the listener what the programme is about and when it is broadcast. Write and hone a script to get the message across succinctly and then record it over a music bed which reflects the type of music you will be playing - for example, for 'Postcard from Spain' I would choose a flamenco guitar track or something equally Spanish and a typical modern country music song for 'Sound of Country'. My trailer for 'Smooth Jazz' starts off a little tongue-in-cheek and goes something like this -

If you like a little late night sax, join me - Vernon Pearce - for Smooth Jazz, a regular programme of laid-back, relaxing, soul and jazz music by artists like Bill Withers, Kenny G and Luther Vandross and with tracks by timeless jazz singers like Diana Krall, Norah Jones and Sade. That's 'Smooth Jazz' coming here soon on Hospital Radio Basingstoke.

This particular trailer is 'vanilla' and doesn't give a time and day, as this varies according to the programme schedule. Other programmes have several trailers, to be used according to the time and day they are broadcast.

You can also widen your audience by writing press releases for local newspapers and magazines. The free press in particular is always hungry for well-written articles and so a brief piece about your new programme or about forthcoming guests appearing on your show, along with a quote from yourself, will generally be well received.

If your station has a website, you can also create a special page for your programme, such as I did with www.hrbasingstoke.co.uk/postcardfromspain. This can give your listeners a foretaste of what is to come in a forthcoming programme, give them more detailed information about your specialist subject or in the case of 'Postcard from Spain', it also provides a record of all the Mediterranean recipes used in my programme. Listeners or fans of your programme can also be allowed to leave comments or pose questions about a show or a particular subject you have aired.

If you are presenting a live programme, emails can also provide an alternative means of communicating with the studio for listeners to make requests or send in answers to on-air quiz questions.

How technology has changed
radio broadcasting

I have been involved in radio broadcasting for less than 15 years but even in that short time I have witnessed major changes brought about by improvements in technology. This has made the whole experience more exciting and I have been proud to watch HRB improving its image, the service it provides to listeners and its output as a result of embracing those changes.

Studio hardware

In the early days, presenters were limited in the range of music they could play by the vinyl record library, supplemented by tape cassettes and then later CDs. Now, computerised music databases, which can be searched and accessed almost instantly, make life very much easier and provide more choice, enabling us to better satisfy patients' requests. More recently, we have supplemented our own music database by taking out a subscription to online supplier Spotify, extending our capabilities even further.

Outside broadcasting

At one time, our live outside broadcast capability extended as far away from the portacabin studio as a microphone cable would reach! The rapidly increasing use of mobile phones, however, meant that presenters could call the studio from an outside event and be 'patched through' to the studio desk, so that listeners could hear reports from a football match on a Saturday afternoon, the Basingstoke Balloon Festival or even the Classic Car Show in the nearby town of Alton and the conversation with the presenter. It was way back in 1991 that we first covered the Basingstoke Carnival using a unit that contained a mobile phone and a place to plug in headphones and a microphone, which in those days was quite new technology. We were later able to record reports from outside events using minidisc and digital recorders.

This mobile technology has been extended to improve communications between presenters and ward visitors around the hospital. Whereas the hospital's internal telephone system was the only method in the past, we are now able to use mobile phones and tablets to provide more interesting programming, where we can interview patients and staff on the wards, allow them to make their requests live on air and chat with the presenter and provide much more interaction. The Saturday morning, live, 'G-floor Jukebox' programme for the children's ward is welcomed by the specialist hospital play leaders as a form of therapy for the youngsters.

Better quality and lower cost links have also been possible using the VOIP technology of Skype and I have described earlier in this book how I have been part of international link-ups with presenters live on air, in some cases sharing in the presentation of a programme as if I was actually in the studio.

Broadcasting over the internet

When I first broadcast my request programme on HRB, it could only be heard by patients and staff in certain parts of the hospital and the principal method of receiving our programmes was via an AM frequency induction loop, originally installed in 1988 within the main hospital building, the signal being received on radios supplied by HRB to certain wards within the range of that loop. These had to be constantly re-tuned and the quality of the AM signal was sometimes poor but in those pre-FM days, listeners were often used to receiving their radio programmes in that way. The induction loop continued in use until 2013.

In 2003, some wards were fitted with bedside radio/ telephone/TV units supplied by an outside contractor Patientline. Now called Hospedia, they have gradually extended their coverage to other parts of the hospital and improved the bedside units they supply to receive FM broadcasts and TV programmes.

However, the biggest advance was HRB's move to broadcasting via the internet, officially launched on the station's 40th anniversary in April 2012, whilst continuing to feed the Hospedia bedside units. With the installation of WiFi within the NHH site, it means that both patients and staff can listen to the station and also communicate with the studio on PCs, laptops, smart phones and tablets, anywhere they can access the internet. It also means that friends and family of patients can listen to requests at home.

Other outside buildings operated by the NHH trust - respite care and convalescent homes, specialist units which care for the mentally ill and so on, which are geographically separate - can also now tune in to HRB. The old AM induction loop was abandoned in January 2013.

Hospital radio is a good place to start

What is a radio presenter? A good place to research the job specifications and qualification for a career in broadcasting is on this website – www.myjobsearch.com/careers/radio-presenter.

Here is a good description of how hospital radio can help you take the first steps in being a radio presenter, which I have taken from a website entitled the Voluntary Worker - www.voluntaryworker.co.uk/hospitalradio -

"Before the explosion of communications and other forms of media courses at universities, websites such as You Tube and innovations like podcasts, hospital radio was seen by those who were active participants within it as possibly one of the few ways in which you could gain the necessary grounding and experience to go on to pursue broadcasting as a career. In fact, many of TV and radio's most established celebrities will have begun their careers with a stint on hospital radio in their formative years.

However, the ethos has changed somewhat these days and, even though it is still good experience for those wishing to enter the broadcasting profession, there are so many other ways and means of doing that these days that it should only be considered as a voluntary job if you intend to simply want to pick up a few skills in a fun environment and are prepared to 'muck in' as opposed to viewing it as your big chance of being the next Chris Evans as, in most cases, you'll end up being disappointed if you intend to view it as a stepping stone to stardom. It can, however, still play some part in providing you with experience should you wish to take it up as a profession in the future."

This is all very true and it is unfair to impose on hospital staff and patient listeners your possibly marginal interest in something like garage music, hip hop or reggae, when the purpose is to entertain them when they are recovering from serious operations or working in difficult jobs. Request programmes will normally be a good indicator of the sort of music your audience wants to hear.

Some well-known broadcasters who started their careers in hospital radio include Ken Bruce, Jill

Dance, Phillip Schofield and Simon Mayo. For many years, Sir Terry Wogan was a great supporter of hospital radio and in fact Patron of the Hospital Broadcasting Association. He was once reported as saying - *"I receive lots of letters from people in hospital, or just out of hospital, telling me of the work you do and the fun you get out of doing it and the good you're doing. You're doing it for nothing, you're doing it because you care but you're also doing it because you love radio, you love broadcasting and I hope you'll continue doing it as you're all doing an enormous amount of good.'*

Acknowledgements

I am extremely grateful to the following people I have mentioned in this book and numerous others I may have omitted, who have helped to make my radio broadcasts so successful and, more importantly, helped me to enjoy the experience.

Talk show guests on WVR and Delta FM

Dr June Chatfield

Tim Brock, Hampshire Fare Officer

Will Grafton, wine expert

Helen Hosker, food expert

Jerry Schooler, Lurgashall Winery

HRB

Neil Ogden, Technical Engineer in the early days at WVR and Programme Controller at Hospital Radio Basingstoke, as well as being my mentor

Nancy Best, the US tourist who was briefly a patient in NHH and Noreen Jonczyk, her American cousin

Marilyn Price, Chairman of HRB and presenter

Sarah Beattie, HRB presenter

Brian Starman, HRB member and co-presenter of 'Grumpy Old Men'

Andrew McCormick, HRB presenter of 'Postcard from New Zealand'

Andy Crabb, short-story writer featured in 'The Lunchbox'

Steve Fox, presenter on Kestrel FM and Breeze FM with whom I linked-up live during HRB's 40th birthday celebrations

Chris Bounds, HRB presenter responsible for broadcasting marathon in 2012

Paul Lefeuvre, one of the founding members of Treloar Hospital Radio, WVR, Delta FM and HRB presenter

Frank Abrams, saxophonist from Swindon and regular guest on 'Smooth Jazz'

Danni Nicholls, singer and songwriter from Bedford, subject of a 'Sound of Country' special

Basingstoke Ladies Choir, subject of a special one hour programme of their concert in conjunction with the Costa Blanca Male Voice Choir

Other mentions

Alan Rowett, radio presenter with many stations including the BBC World Service

Tony Dean, DJ on the Costa Blanca and currently presenter on Pure Gold FM

Ex-F1 racing driver Jody Scheckter

TV chef James Martin

......and not forgetting my wife Celia who helped tirelessly with all the proof reading